Deliver Me from Negative Self Talk
A Guide to Speaking Faith-filled Words

Lynn R. Davis

PUBLISHED BY:
Lynn R Davis
Copyright © 2012
http://Lynnrdavis.com

D1300836

TABLE OF CONTENTS

Talking Guide Example:

Don't say: "My entire body aches. I'm just falling apart!"

Do Say: Sickness and disease shall not lord over me.

Preface

Satan deliberately attacked Job's family, his possessions, and his physical health.

Sometimes the problems we face are direct attacks from the enemy. But other times, we have ourselves to blame. We curse ourselves by speaking words of doom and death.

Words should be chosen carefully, because they have power to give life and to destroy it.

Negative self talk is conceived in the mind and birthed through our speech. But just as negative seeds produce negative harvest, so will the seeds of God's word, planted in a faithful heart, produce an abundant harvest of blessings.

Introduction:

Proverbs 18: 21 says, "Life and death are in the power of the tongue." Simply put, our words will either give life or cause death. Where did we get this powerful gift?

From our Father that's where. Just as God created the heavens and the earth by speaking words, we too can create the life we desire for ourselves.

Here's an easy formula to remember:

MEDITATION + DECLARATION = MANIFESTATION

If you want something to happen in your life, speak it into existence. Instead of talking about how terrible your relationship is, confess that the relationship is Godly and all is well.

Be Careful What You Say

When you are upset or angry, resist the temptation to feed the fire of doom with negative words. No matter how broke you are, don't go around saying, "I'm broke".

Instead, you say, "All of my needs are met in Jesus name. When you speak what you want, you are calling it into existence.

Even though it seems that nothing is happening in the natural, things are changing in the spirit realm.

And it's only a matter of time before your situation improves. "Calling those things that be not as though they were", is a biblical principal.

We have been given the power to speak into existence God's desire for our lives. That is why we should be very careful how we respond to even the simplest challenges in our lives.

Once we realize the seriousness of our words, we begin to choose them more carefully. Okay, now that we have our own words under control, let's discuss the next important issue—the words that other people say to us.

Sticks And Stones Break Bones And Words Do Hurt!

Most of the words we hear seem innocent and even humorous. But remember what we said before; words either give life or cause death. "Sticks and stones may break my bones, but words will never hurt me".

We said it all the time as kids. But the truth is; words can hurt. At work I was sharing with a co-worker how I had just been diagnosed with high blood pressure.

His immediate response was, "Be careful. You could stroke out and die." At first I laughed it off. "Boy you're so crazy."

But, later that day, I started thinking about what he said. It was true that extreme stress could increase blood pressure and even lead to a stroke.

I had been experiencing a little numbness- maybe even a little fatigue and dizziness? The negative thoughts started running rampant in my mind.

Honestly, before hearing my friend's "words of wisdom", emphasis on "**_dom_**"; having a stroke had never entered my mind. He spoke the words.

I meditated on his negativity, and voila! I started experiencing symptoms. Ever heard of hypochondria? The American Century Dictionary defines it as an abnormal anxiety about one's health.

My grandmother was accused of being a hypochondriac. She was always experiencing multiple types of illnesses.

Even though doctors couldn't find anything wrong, bottles of prescriptions lined her dresser. Eighty percent of her day was spent in bed.

Granny only got out of the house for doctor's appointments. Friends and neighbors visited with their stories of doom and gloom. They're words were feeding her fear of death by illness.

If only she had known the power that she had within her to speak health and healing into her life; to control her anxiety; and call forth a sound mind and peace.

Granny had the fiery darts of negativity shooting at her

from all directions—both from within and from the gloomy people around her.

What's my point? She meditated on the thoughts and like seeds they took root and produced fear. The fear produced doubt. And doubt murders faith.

The constant meditating on negativity lead to her taking multiple medications, but never to her being healed. As believers we must not allow negativity to overcome us.

Read Paul's instructions to the church: "For the weapons of our warfare are not carnal but mighty in God for pulling down strongholds, casting down arguments and every high thing that exalts itself against the knowledge of God and to bring every thought into captivity" 2 Cor. 10:4-5.

We have to capture bad thoughts and control them with the word of God. The only way to win a spiritual battle is to fight it using spiritual weapons.

"(3) We are human, but we don't wage war as humans do. (4) We use God's mighty weapons, not worldly weapons, to knock down the strongholds of human reasoning and to destroy false arguments." (2 Cor. 10 NLV)

If I hadn't come to myself and remembered that Jesus died that I might have life, I would have meditated my way right into a stroke.

How could this happen?

MEDITATION + DECLARATION = MANIFESTATION

It's a process. First, you see or hear something negative. Next, you think about it or meditate on it (too long).

Then, you start speaking about the negative thing you saw or heard. Finally, the negativity overcomes you and you begin to feel like there is no hope.

No Matter How Bad It Looks Stay Positive

Let's say you're having relationship issues. Like most people, you want to vent. So you talk to your friends about your situation. Of course, as your friends, they're going to take your side.

They begin to say negative things about your situation like, "She's never going to change". "Just leave". "You deserve better". All of these seeds are planted in your mind just waiting to be watered with fear so that they can grow and produce division and dissolution.

You've now developed a totally pessimistic attitude toward that person and your relationship. And if you allow, the situation will end in pain. What will you do?

Will you fight with spiritual weapons or will you lay down in defeat? You could respond either way.

But let's look at the spiritual approach. First recognize that Satan hates unity and is working to destroy your relationship. Why does he hate unity?
 Because God blesses unity!

Read Psalms 133:1 -3. "(v1) Behold how good and how pleasant it is for brethren to dwell together in unity. (v3) It is like the dew of Hermon Descending upon the mountains of Zion' for there the Lord commanded the blessing-Life forevermore."

We've looked at the spiritual approach. So maybe you're wondering what the negative approach look like? Here goes:

You hear your friend's words. You meditated on the negative aspects of your relationship. You start speaking negatively. Your relationship ends.

Short and sweet-once again, whatever you meditate on will manifest.

Revisit the formula:

MEDITATION+ DECLARATION= MANIFESTATION.

That's why God wants us to meditate on His word day and night. And Romans 10:17 tells us that "faith comes by hearing, and hearing by the word of God".

Make God's Words Your Words

As believers, we must speak only words of prosperity, health, and power. It takes some practice. But it can be done. Study the word and meditate on God's promises.

Soon, instead of words of despair flowing from your lips, you will begin to flood your life with God's perfect will!

And what started out as practice will be as common as breathing!

Say the formula aloud:

MEDITATION + DECLARATION= MANIFESTATION

1- Words You Should Never Speak About Yourself

Admit it. You talk to yourself.

I talk to myself all the time. I especially do it when I'm zooming around the house. I remind myself, "don't forget the fabric softener" or scold myself, "Lynn, you put it on the list and still forgot to buy it!"

Of course, these are some of the nicer conversations I have with myself.

And most of the time, self-talk is pretty harmless. No one gets offended and nobody gets hurt.

But when a situation is more serious than staticky underwear or a crusty oven racks things change; the voices of panic and fear take over.

Like the day you blow a job interview; lose a loved one; or get devastating news from the doctor. The voices change and innocent self-talk turns negative and critical.

We make comments like, "I give up. I can't do it." "I can't go on without them" and "I'll be dead in six months."

Negative thoughts are spiritually impure and must be filtered. The word of God is your filter. Any such thought that makes you feel defeated, hurt, or insufficient is a **LIE** and must be filtered through the word of God.

Study for knowledge. Seek understanding. Pray for wisdom. Find out what the bible says about your situation. Remember, "Seek and you will find".

Your goal is to get to the truth. It is the truth that will set you free!

Your Personal Speaking Guide

1. **Don't say**: "My entire body aches. I'm just falling apart!"

Do Say: Sickness and disease shall not lord over me.

2. **Don't say**: "I am so exhausted. I really don't feel like doing anything today."

Do Say: I can do all things through Christ who strengthens me

3. **Don't say**: "This headache is killing me!"

Do Say: Headache, I resist you in the name of Jesus and by his stripes I am healed and made whole.

4. **Don't say**: "I can't do that. I'm too scared. What if I fail?"

Do Say: I am courageous. God has not given me a spirit of fear but of a sound mind, power and love.

5. **Don't say**: "I'm always broke."

Do Say: I am abundantly supplied. God is supplying all of my needs according to his riches in glory.

6. **Don't say**: "I am so depressed."

Do Say: I have the mind of Christ and the peace of God that surpasses all understanding.

7. **Don't say**: "I just can't stop this bad habit."

Do Say: I am not tempted or tried above that which I am able to overcome. I am more than a conqueror.

8. **Don't say**: "Everyone in my family has this problem. It's hereditary, so I will probably have the same problems too."

Do Say: Christ redeemed me from the curse, being made a curse himself. I am delivered out of every affliction.

9. **Don't say**: "I don't like people. I'd rather be alone, besides people are mean."

Do Say: I have the compassion of Christ in my heart and I love all people.

10. **Don't say**: "I'll never meet this deadline. My work is overwhelming me, there's no way that I can meet the demands of this job."

Do Say: I have the grace to overcome every obstacle. God is giving me wisdom to solve every problem that I am faced with.

11. **Don't Say**: I'm happy with what I have. Why should I want more?

Do Say: Jesus came that I might have abundant life. I am blessed to be a blessing to others.

12. **Don't say**: "I will never get married. No one wants to marry me."

Do Say: God is preparing me for marriage and he is raising up the perfect mate for me.

13. **Don't Say**: God is not answering my prayers so maybe he's not listening.

Do Say: God is mindful of me and he hears me when I pray.

14. **Don't Say**: "Everything is getting on my nerves and I am going crazy!"

Do Say: I will think only of things that are lovely, good, just and have good report so that the peace of God dwells in me.

15. **Don't say**: "I'm so angry. I will never be able to forgive."

Do Say: The joy of the Lord is my strength. My heart is filled with the compassion of Christ and I forgive those who trespass against me.

16. **Don't say**: "My Company is going to have a reduction in force. I know what I'm going to do if I get laid off."

Do Say: When one door closes God has to open another

door.

17. **Don't say**: "I am lonely. I wish I had someone to in my life."

Do Say: I am complete in Christ. I am never lonely because he is always with me.

18. **Don't say**: "Things will never get better. I may as well give up."

Do Say: Eyes haven't seen what God has prepared for me and in due season I shall reap, if I faint not.

19. **Don't say**: "The weather is terrible. I hope I don't have an accident."

Do Say: The angels of the Lord are encamped around me and not hurt or harm shall come near me.

20. **Don't say**: "I'm too old to change. You can't teach old dogs new tricks."

Do Say: I am a new creature. Old things have passed away.

21. **Don't Say:** "Everyone else is doing it, why shouldn't I?"

Do Say: God has called me out of darkness and into his marvelous light. I am in this world but I am not of this world.

22. **Don't say**: "I can't help gossiping. My friends encourage it."

Do Say: I will not participate in gossip. Corrupt communication brings destruction.

23. **Don't say**: "No one cares about me!"

Do Say: God loves me and he is Jehovah-Shammah" (The Lord Is There)

2-Words You Should Never Speak About Others

As a mother of a recovering addict, I know this principle is a tough one. When I first found out that my son was smoking pot in high school I lost it.

I used words I've never used in my life. I was so angry you could have fried on egg on my head!

I was disappointed in him. Angry that I'd missed the signs and appalled that the enemy had the nerve to go after my child. Not my son! (Maybe that's a book for another time.)

Every chance I got I shared my disgust and contempt for his rebellion. I told family and coworkers how much trouble he was getting into and how many times he'd been arrested.

I complained and lamented till I was out of breath, then had the nerve to pray to God for change. What I should have been doing was praying for him, with him, and speaking words of promise over his life. While keeping my mouth closed about what was happening.

The more negatively I spoke about his habits and his choices, the more he backed away from me and toward the rebellion. It wasn't until I took my negative thoughts into captivity and changed my words, that I began to see change and have been blessed to witness his deliverance.

Learn from my mistakes. Don't speak negativity over the people in your life. If you truly care about them and want to reconcile the relationship, replace your negative perceptions and comments with the word of God.

Remember, "For our struggle is not against human opponents, but against rulers, authorities, cosmic powers in the darkness around us..." (Eph 6:12)

Your Personal Speaking Guide

1. **Don't say:** "My supervisor hates me; my co-workers are messy & I hate this job!"

Do Say: I love those who hate me and I will do well to those who misuse me. No weapon formed against me shall prosper. The battle is the Lords.

2. **Don't say**: "My children do not listen to a word that I say. They are just bad."

Do Say: My child is a blessing from the lord. My child obeys the word of God and honors his mother and father.

3. **Don't say**: "My husband is lazy and worthless. I don't know why I married him."

Do Say: My husband is a righteous man of God and he loves me like
Christ loves the church.

4. **Don't say**: "My in-laws are incorrigible and they are making my life miserable."

Do Say: My in-laws are transformed by the renewing of their mind. I am an example for them and they will see my good works and glorify the Father in heaven.

5. **Don't say**: "People in church are cruel. I'm never going to church again."

Do Say: God has many great churches and he is revealing

to me the church that I should attend.

6. **Don't say**: "My child makes terrible grades in school. He or she will never amount to anything."

Do Say: God has a purpose for my child. My child is royal priesthood and has the wisdom of Daniel and the favor of God and man. My child is empowered to prosper.

7. **Don't Say**: "Why does he or she behave that way? They're just crazy."

 Do Say: Christ alone is perfect.

3- Words You Should Never Allow Others to Speak About You

Some people are just plain negative. That's all there is to it. But you don't have to allow them to discourage you. Regardless of whom they are or how close they may be to us.

Sometimes the people closest to you are the one who will be the least supportive and the most negative.

You're all excited about your knew goal and you share it with your significant other, brother, sister, BFF, and you're met with negativity.

That's the last thing you expected. How are you supposed to process that? What do you do?

You ignore negative people. That's what you do.

I deal with people and their toxic comments all the time regarding my health and weight loss goals.

Anyone who knows me is aware that I'm an advocate of health and fitness. You would think people would appreciate that, right?

Wrong!

I hear comments all the time like "You're going to be too skinny", "You don't need to lose weight" or "I can't eat like that. I love food too much." on and on...

Did I let that stop me from dropping 4 jean sizes and getting healthy? No. I did not. And I will not. I prefer not spending hundreds of dollars a year on high blood pressure pills and asthma pumps- thank you very much.

You see, I'm fully aware that negative people are speaking from the depths of their own insecurity and self-doubt.

So I brush it off.

That's what I want to encourage you to do as well. When you decide to improve yourself, there will be people who will say and do things to discourage you.

I encourage you to shake those negative people off. Realize they are only projecting their lack of discipline and lack of motivation on to you.

"Hurting people hurt people". I don't know who said that, but it is certainly a true statement.

Some people are unhappy with themselves and they're jealous of your drive and commitment to self improvement. *How dare you improve your quality of life? Who do you think you are?*

You can't please negative people. They are unhappy no matter what. They speak negative no matter what. They gossip about you when you fail and they rain on your parade when you succeed.

There's no pleasing them. So stop trying! Simply smile and keep it moving.

You have goals. Don't let negative people deter you. Stay focused and you will succeed.

"Let no corrupt communication proceed out of your mouth, but that which is good to the use of edifying, that it may minister grace unto the hearers. (Ephesians 4:29)

If the words that people are speaking over you make you don't uplift you or encourage you do better, then you should never receive them as truth.

Your Personal Speaking Guide

1. **What they say:** "You poor thing."
Response: I am blessed and I have the grace to overcome anything!

2. **What they say**: "How do you plan to acquire that? You don't make enough."

Response: I am abundantly supplied. I am not moved by what I see. It's only temporary.

3. **What they say**: "That's a terrible sickness; you could die from it."

Response: I am healed. I shall live and not die.

4. **What they say**: "You don't look well. Are you sick?"

Response: I have divine health. I resist sickness in the name of Jesus.

5. **What they say**: "Yeah right, do you really believe you're going to pull that off?"

Response: I can do all things through Christ who strengthens me.

6. **What they say**: "If I were you, I would be so depressed."

Response: God has not given me the spirit of fear, but of a sound mind, power, and love.

7. **What they say**: "I could never give that much money to the church. I have bills to pay."

Response: When I give, God causes men to give to me, press down, shaken together and running over. God supplies all of my needs according to his riches in glory.

8. **What they say**: "I don't believe in anything that I can't see."

Response: Without faith it is impossible to please God. I receive the promised of God through faith.

9. **What they say**: "Don't you get tired of cooking, cleaning and taking care of everyone else?"

Response: I have the grace to care for the family that God has blessed me with.

4-Words You Should Never Speak About God

God Is Not Angry With You

One of the most difficult things for us to believe as Christians is that God is not mad at us. We condemn ourselves because of our past sins or even our present mistakes.

The danger in believing that you serve a **mad God** is that you will begin to feel you do not deserve God's goodness or His blessings. In turn you will begin to doubt and have fear.

While we don't condone sin or even encourage it, we do know that the bible tells us in Romans 8 "...*there is no condemnation for those who belong to Christ Jesus...*"

I posted a word of encouragement on my Facebook page that I believe applies to this chapter...

"Regardless of disagreements among siblings and family, when an outsider threatens a family member, we rise against that attacker to protect them. Though your actions don't always please God, when the enemy threatens to destroy you, God raises a standard against him to protect you. You have protection. Not because you do everything right, but because you are in God's family. Receive it by faith."

You are part of the family of God. He loves you and wants to protect you. Here are some daily confessions based on Romans 8 and Isaiah 54.

Meditating on these truths will help you to address your feelings of condemnation and fears of inadequacy because you incorrectly believe that God is angry with you:

*I have an unconditional covenant with God.

*God loves me and He has reconciled me unto himself.

*God is not angry with me. He loves me.

*The mountains and the hills will pass away before God's covenant   promise to love me and give me peace can ever be broken.

*God has sworn never to rebuke me or to be angry with me.

*God's covenant of peace will never leave me.

*God's unfailing love and peace for me will never be shaken.

*My righteousness is of the Lord. I am not condemned. I am loved by God.

Make these confessions daily and know that God loves you regardless of your past, present, or future mistakes. Seek to do good and please Him with your life.

Allow His love to fill your heart and overflow in your life. You do not serve a mad God.

Meditate on Isaiah 54: 10, "Though the mountains be shaken and the hills be removed, yet my unfailing love for you will not be shaken nor my covenant of peace be removed," says the LORD, who has compassion on you."

You serve a loving God. Hills will be removed and mountains shaken before God's love will ever be taken away from you or His covenant with you broken. Believe that. Receive it and walk in victory.

That said here are a few examples of words you should never speak about God.

1. "God Doesn't Love Me."

2. "God is too busy for my problems."

3. "My problems are too big for God."

4. "I'm alone. God is not there."

5. "God can't heal my disease."

6. "God is going to punish me for my sins."

These are lies, lies, lies, all lies.

The Devil is a liar. He is the "Father of Lies" (John 8:44)

Satan is destined to eternal damnation. He is damned. And he wants to take as many lost souls with him as he possibly can.

Don't let the bad things in life make you believe God doesn't love you.

God is love. And God loves us--with all of our issues and faults. Jehovah is not waiting to condemn you or to punish you. He wants to bless you.

He's waiting to help you and heal the hurt. It doesn't matter how much wrong you've done. Or how many mistakes you've made or will make.

He only wants to bless you. He is mindful of you and no human could ever love you as much as He does!

God is your provider, peace, and healer. He wants the best for you. And you have to get into the habit of talking like it.

One thing that will help, is meditating on the names of God. Learning who He is will help you understand His character and how much He loves and wants you to succeed in life.

5- Knowing God's Loving Character

"O LORD, our Lord, How excellent is Your **name** *in all the earth…" Psalm 8:1*

When you know who God is, you can't help but feel comforted and empowered. Everything that you could possibly need is in the Father.

He IS whatever you need Him to be. And He is waiting for you to come to Him.

Whatever you need God IS! God told Moses in Exodus "I am that I am." Don't put limits on Gods ability to heal your body, or repair your broken heart.

God loves you and wants to you to be prosperous in every area of your life.

Before you allow someone to tell you that God doesn't love you or that He cannot help you, remember the words, "I am that I am."

He is love, provision, protection, peace, healing, etc. The list goes on and on. Let's take a look at some of the most common characteristics of God our Father:

Names of Jehovah God

1. Adonai: My Master

2. El Elyon: The Most High God

3. El Olam: The Everlasting Father

4. El Roi: My God Sees All

5. El Shaddai: My All-Sufficient God

6. Elohim: My Creator

7. Jehovah-Jireh: The LORD my Provider

8. Jehovah-Mekoddishkem: The LORD Who sanctifies me

9. Jehovah-Nissi: The LORD My Banner

10. Jehovah-Raah: The LORD My Shepherd

11. Jehovah-Rapha: The LORD That Heals me

12. Jehovah-Sabaoth: The LORD of Hosts

13. Jehovah-Shalom: The LORD my Peace

14. Jehovah-Shammah: The LORD Is Always There

15. Jehovah-Tsidkenu: The LORD my Righteousness

God is your creator. He loves you. He wants to provide for you. His desire is to heal you and bring you peace in your storms.

You are righteous because of His son Jesus. And He is always with you even at this moment.

There is no need to speak doom and gloom. God has a good plan for your life. The problems you are facing come from the enemy, not the Father (Jeremiah 29:11).

When you know God, you know His nature. By nature, God is love. And that love is unconditional for believers in Jesus Christ.

I hope that you've been blessed. And I could say that this is the end, but it's not, it's only the beginning. Go forth. "Call those things that be not as though they were." (Romans 4:17)

Choose your words carefully from this day forward. Use them to create a life that you enjoy living.

Remember:

MEDITATION + DECLARATION= MANIFESTATION

Dismiss negative thoughts, words, and feelings. Study your Father's character. Meditate on His word. Declare it. And watch your life change for the better.

6-Daily Inspiration and Scripture Meditation

Ever heard the saying, "What's in you will come out?"
It's a true saying.

The only way that we can consistently speak faith-filled
words is if those words are "in us" or abundant in our
hearts. Matthew 12:34, "For out of the abundance of the
heart the mouth speaks."

And for God's word to flourish in our hearts, we must sow
seeds of the word through daily prayer, mediation, and
study.

The word of God in our hearts takes root and produces a
bumper crop of manifestation and breakthrough. So that
when we open our mouths to speak, faith-filled words will
overflow from it.

Actively seek God's guidance and practice speaking faith-
filled words daily. It may feel forced or "fake" at first. And
you may be tempted to give up, but please don't.

The pages that follow include 7 days of inspiration and
scripture meditation. During your study time mediate on
them and pray for understanding.

Ask the Holy Spirit to reveal the value and meaning to you
for your life and to show you the areas you need to
strengthen.

Matthew 7: 7 – *"Ask, and it shall be given you; seek, and
ye shall find; knock, and it shall be opened unto you:"*

SCRIPTURE MEDITATION

AND

WORDS OF INSPIRATION

DAY 1

Scripture Meditation:

Proverbs 18:21 -"Death and life are in the power of the tongue: and they that love it shall eat the fruit thereof."

Thought for today:

Your words can kill or give life. And there are consequences for both. Today make an effort to speak words that give life and hope for a new beginning to a coworker, friend or family member.

Inspirational Quote:

"A helping word to one in trouble is often like a switch on a railroad track an inch between wreck and smooth, rolling prosperity."

-Henry Ward Beecher

DAY 2

Scripture Meditation:

Proverbs 21:23(NLT)- "Watch your tongue and keep your mouth shut, and you will stay out of trouble."

Thought for today:

"If you can't say something nice, don't say anything at all." We don't always have to talk. Sometimes, it's better to keep quiet especially to avoid starting trouble. If your words will cause confusion don't just blurt them out. Let the Holy Spirit guide you. "God is not the author of confusion but of peace" (1 Corinthians 14:33).

Inspirational Quote:

"If a sudden jar can cause me to speak an impatient, unloving word, then I know nothing of Calvary love. For a cup brimful of sweet water cannot spill even one drop of bitter water, however suddenly jolted."

-Amy Carmichael

DAY 3

Scripture Meditation

 1 Corinthians 2:16-"Who can know the Lord's thoughts? Who knows enough to teach them? But we understand these things, for we have the mind of Christ."

Thought for today:

As a believer you have access to the God's thoughts-through His Son, His word and His Spirit. As we spend time with God, our relationship with Him matures. And we begin to gain insight and understanding concerning His good plans for our lives. Pray and believe for the mind of Chris. Then allow God's thoughts to lead your actions.

Inspirational Quote:

"We need, men so possessed by the Spirit of God that God can think His thoughts through our minds, that He can plan His will through our actions, that He can direct His strategy of world evangelization through His Church."

-Alan Redpath

DAY 4

Scripture Mediation:

Matthew 21:22 -"And whatever you ask in prayer, you will receive, if you have faith."

Thought for today:

There will be times when it seems impossible to overcome what you face. With God nothing is impossible. Your faith is the key to overcoming. Don't mediate on doubtful thoughts or speak doubtful words. Doubt turns to unbelief. And it is unbelief that drives a wedge between you and your promised victory. Stand fast on God's word. His word cannot fail.

Inspirational Quote:

"Daily living by faith on Christ is what makes the difference between the sickly and the healthy Christian, between the defeated and the victorious saint."

-A.W.Pink

DAY 5

Scripture Meditation:

Joshua 1: 8 - "This Book of the Law shall not depart from your mouth, but you shall meditate on it day and night, so that you may be careful to do according to all that is written in it. For then you will make your way prosperous, and then you will have good success."

Thought for today: We are no longer under the law, but covered by grace. However, I believe the principle is that we should not make the mistake of waiting for God to bring us success. He has already blessed us with the greatest success conduit- His son Jesus Christ. To receive the success that is promised to us we must first receive Jesus into our lives as Lord and savior. Then by faith believe that we have also received salvation, healing, prosperity, and wholeness. Meditate on the promises in God's word. Learn them. Believe them. Declare them. And then you "will have good success".

Inspirational Quote:

"The foundation stones for a balanced success are honesty, character, integrity, faith, love and loyalty."

-Zig Ziglar

Day 6

Scripture Meditation:

Isaiah 26:3-4 "You keep him in perfect peace whose mind is stayed on you, because he trusts in you. Trust in the Lord forever, for the Lord God is an everlasting rock:"

Thought for today:

As the hymn says, we often forfeit our peace because we fail to take our problems to God. God wants us to cast our cares on him. Not our unbelieving neighbors, disgruntled coworkers, or pessimistic family members. Though everything around you seems to be falling apart, take heart in knowing that God's word is not. It is solid as an everlasting rock. His word and His love are will never fade. He is a part of you. And that part of you is indestructible. It's the part of your life that rebuilds, restores, and resurrects! Nothing is impossible with God.

Inspirational Scripture:

"You were made by God and for God and until you understand that, life will never make sense."

— Rick Warren

Day 7

Scripture Meditation:

1 John 4:4- "Because greater is He that is in you than He that is in the world."

Thought for today:

The word and Jesus are one. "In the beginning was the word. The word was God and the word was with God." (John 1:1) Jesus lives in you. And He that lives in you is greater and more powerful than any obstacle you face in the world. Don't look down at your problems. Look up at the promise. Your help comes from the Lord and He is high and lifted up, just as your countenance should be. Keep your head up.

Inspirational Quote:

"If there be anything that can render the soul calm, dissipate its scruples and dispel its fears, sweeten its sufferings by the anointing of love, impart strength to all its actions, and spread abroad the joy of the Holy Spirit in its countenance and words, it is this simple and childlike repose in the arms of God."

-S.D. Gordon

This may be the end of the book, but it is just the beginning of a beautiful new positive life for you and the lives your faith will bless.

God bless and thank you so much for the support.

Coming soon…

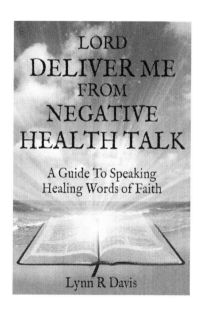

LORD DELIVER ME FROM NEGATIVE HEALTH TALK:

A GUIDE TO SPEAKING HEALING WORDS OF FAITH

MAY ALSO ENJOY:

GET OFF YOUR KNEES AND DO SOMETHING ABOUT IT:

17 THINGS TO DO AFTER YOU PRAY

CONNECT WITH ME AT: http://Lynnrdavis.com or email me at lynnrdavis@hotmail.com

23327796R00026

Made in the USA
Lexington, KY
06 June 2013